CAN I ASK YOU A QUESTION ?

Edited by Henry J. Lindley

Published and printed in the
United States Of America

FOREWORD

I have been in the sales arena for over 30 years, three decades. When you say it like that, it seems monolithic, but in that time I have come to one great truth, and though it may be hard to swallow, it is simply put this way: the inescapable conclusion is that 90% of the people in this profession are not great salespeople.

My next conclusion must follow that 10% of the salespeople are doing 90% of the selling. Yes, this is hard to explain, and even harder to accept, but it is the truth. It seems to me that everyone in their respected fields think they are the experts. I see very little humility and willingness to get better in a field that people call their profession. I believe there are plenty of good salespeople, but very few of what I call "Rainmakers". These people share all the same characteristics and same mannerisms. They are not very detail-oriented, and they are usually the life of the party. It is a fact that we as salespeople are conduits for information, even if that information doesn't rise to the level of engineering specs.

The "Rainmakers", most of all, enjoy what they are doing, and it is critical they are social. Being **_social_**, in the old sense of the word, not always connected to the word media, is the driving force in their lives. The truth be told, a truly social connection is what will drive the sale.

We called this being **_"a people person"_** thirty years ago. I have been so upset in the corporate world that I wanted to write a book that will successfully train people to be true sales professionals.

This book is a simple read but contains the proper fundamentals to increase your sales, and therefore you become more successful. It can serve as a guide to help you develop a skill set that will make you marketable within the workforce. I have had the desire to share this information with sales professionals for a long time and believe the time is right to help people be better and more proficient in this critical profession. Though we are not always treated as such, it is my hope that this book will be a roadmap to help you become more professional.

Truly, I believe that most people want to get better, sell better, and become those "rainmakers" but do not know how. It is difficult to write a book of fundamentals when most salespeople hate to read. No use to deny this fact! You probably have a stack of **"How to Sell"** books piled up on the floor at home. <u>But this won't be one of those!</u>

This book will give you the straight story, and you will find it to be helpful, meaningful, and to have a real impact in and with your occupation. The information contained in this volume will make you infinitely more successful, as it has made me in every facet of my sales career. I understand the basics of sales because I live them every day. I know all salespeople are skeptical, but here it is in a nutshell: **"As a sales professional, get involved with that customer!"**

The customer will tell you everything you need to know; you only have to ask (and listen). The customer knows what he or she needs and knows just what he or she needs to hear from the salesperson in order to solve their problem. Our job is to *"hear"* that solution. How do we hear? Glad you asked! We ask questions.

Why do we find it so difficult to ask questions? Why is it that somehow asking questions diminishes us as sales professionals? Isn't it our job to ascertain what our customer needs? We, as sales professionals, want to make statements. All salespeople have stories and big personalities that are a large part of the reason we are successful.

We want to tell our clients how good our product is, the special price we have compared to our inferior competition---what unique benefits and features they offer. The truth about the whole process is that your customer really does not care. *"Did he just say that?"* you asked; let me explain. The customer cares about what is in it for them. How does it affect the customer personally or professionally? How can you solve their problem right now? Selling is not always a solution business. We will return to this later...

I have lived by the simple premise to **leave people better than you find them**. This includes your customers, their markets and or problems. I know that everyone has a story and they want to tell it. It is our job to listen to that story and be **engaged**; that is "active listening". I not only listen--- I hear.

Active Listening is one of the fundamentals of selling. You need to process that information and discern the components that will help you build value. I tell salespeople all the time that people's perceptions are their realities. They believe what is on the surface and do not drill down. It is amazing to me that when you really care about a customer, the selling process becomes simple. You are helping that person. I have never had a hidden agenda and really like social interaction. Helping our customers seems to be the most natural practice in our profession.

Another great thing about selling is you get paid to meet people. The more you get yourself out there, the more opportunity you have to close business. We will discuss the simple fundamentals on how to **hear** your customer and to get them to tell you how you can help them purchase your product.

I guarantee after you read this book, you will have more marketable skills that other companies will want to help produce results for them.

You will also be able to teach these skills and get a better position or generate more income for your family. Most of these ideas will be a paradigm shift and exactly the opposite of how you have been taught in the sales arena. I have been in the profession for over 30 years, and until I was taught these skills, I was doing what 90% of your competition is doing at the moment. I ask you to have an open mind and jump into this exciting and rewarding way to this new sales process. These short chapters are skill sets that will pay huge dividends in the long run. You have to remember, this is an investment that will be with you the rest of your life.

These things are also life lessons that you will not have to go through. I have made the mistakes and will teach you how not to make them. We need to start the sales process with an open mind and stay on track. You have to remember, you are asking questions to help your customer and yourself. There are no shortcuts in this process, and I guarantee you will enjoy talking with your customer. I hope you start doing these simple ten things daily. I promise you will be more successful in this profession.

Chapters

Chapter 1
Be Responsive

You should always start with first things first. I'll admit, I struggled on how I should start my book and always kept coming back to how the great salespeople are setting themselves apart from their counterparts. What made me different from my colleagues? I know this is simplistic, but it definitely was the difference. In a world of iPhones®, iPads®, Droids™, Laptops, Email, and phone text, we are still poor communicators. We can Facebook® someone instantly but cannot answer a phone call from work. I cannot tell you how many times I notice salespeople, managers, and co-workers intentionally sending calls straight to voicemail. When I see this happening, I always asked myself, "*Do they do this to me?*" The answer was yes! You shouldn't even have to ask, and don't kid yourself that you are the exception.

I promise you that if you are not getting back with your customer, someone else will, or already has. Your customer wants instant gratification. They need something when they are calling you. I have received more purchase orders because my competition would not get back in touch with a customer. I have learned this lesson the hard way. I have lost numerous sales because I did not get back in touch with the customer.

I met perhaps one of the best salespeople ever about five years ago. I asked him to teach me his business. Don "Cotton" Coltharp is his name. He started his days around 5 am. When I rode with him and met his customers, they all loved him!

Even to this day, I have not heard a single bad or derogatory word about him. One day, I asked him why he has been so successful in his field. "**Response**" was his only reply. He had a black book, and he wrote everything down, and this may shock some of you, *he always answered his phone.*

He completed every task on his list by the end of the day. If the customer needed him, he drove there the next day. He said it was simple (Cotton is a very humble guy). He loves to hear their story. I could not agree more.

When a salesperson is remiss in getting back to you, they are inadvertently asking you to become patient and operate on their timetable. The customer may also feel diminished by a lack of response. Do you think a customer that feels diminished is more likely or less likely to buy from your competition?

A quick response is one of the most vital keys of starting the sales process and **developing a relationship** with your customer.

This is one of those things that are simple to duplicate, so that is just what I did! I delivered the product when they ordered it. I did not wait. I went out to see my customers every week. You have heard the old adage, *"Out of sight, out of mind."* When you are interested in your customers, they want to see you. My best advice to my sales staff was, **<u>"See the people, see the people, and see the people."</u>**

Could it be so simple in such a complex world? Why are other salespeople not responsive? If you commit to a simple fundamental such as the one I learned from Mr. Coltharp, you will be successful. **Be Responsive***!* (Your competition may have read my book!)

You have to get out and "cultivate the soil". A vast majority of salespeople are "order takers". They are **reactive instead of proactive.** They hate to make cold calls, and they hate to travel. The most successful people I have worked with hated the office. They were on the road. They wanted their phone to ring. I hear salespeople all the time say they want to be busy, but they do not mean it. Why would you not want to be so busy that there is not enough time in the day to handle all tasks? The money will definitely follow the chaos. It is your job to organize the many moving parts and check the boxes.

This has simple implications. Your manager is a taskmaster, and you need to get his box checked. Your time is better spent serving customers than the minutiae of a spreadsheet. Paperwork must be done, but your main concern is the customer.

In the same vein, you do not need to let your manager know you are combative when it comes to their priorities. Organization is a must, but relationships outweigh a spreadsheet or any CRM (Customer Relationship Management) software any day (no matter how good the program).

You must prioritize the day and make sure all the details are complete. The main problem here is that the best salespeople are unorganized. It is part of their personality, and because of this they have to force themselves to check the box. It is hard to explain, but being **social, i.e. relationships,** is more important to them than checking that box.

The best salespeople find a way to merge the two. Some have said a messy desk is the sign of an active mind. While there is little proof to substantiate this, if your desk is messy and your sales are sky-high, your manager is not likely to say anything to you. The rainmakers' personality makes them naturally unorganized. I always say **<u>volume hides a multitude of sins</u>**. We grant leniency to salespeople who are truly selling. It is amazing that we do not feel the importance of our CRM when deals are being closed. Why? This is simple--- we know they are following up if their numbers are great.

Poor performers are always micromanaged. I believe in the exact opposite. We need to let the poor performers shadow our "**A**" players. When we start to micromanage, our team starts to just shut down. They reach the point that they are so afraid of making the wrong move, they make no move at all. This is called *"paralyzation by analyzation"*.

We need to spend quality time with our lower performing sales team to create a genuine level of trust. This trust will get us to the real truth of why they are falling short of their goals. This is really important on working hard to developing an inclusive relationship with your sales team.

Let's examine the component parts of a great sales team.

If you watch a great football team, you can see all the moving parts, the wheels and the cogs, if you will. The coach has an offensive coordinator and a defensive coordinator. He knows how to properly delegate. It is very hard to learn to delegate when we often feel like we can trust ourselves to do the task at hand. The reason for this is that we want to be sure it is done correctly. However, we cannot do it all, and we cannot do it better and faster than the team. The truth is, we need to learn and recognize "the what and where" and "the strengths and weaknesses" of our team. The ability to **be responsive** is a highly important trait to a sales professional on the upswing. When we are responsive, we make it rain.

If you are highly responsive, you will need help, and you will have to delegate. You must have confidence in your team (we will discuss building a team later on, and how to trust people with customers).

The customer is calling most of the time because they need something. It is very simple if you take the call. It is my opinion that a quick response will pay dividends in the long term. You must have a task list and check if off by the end of the day. Juggling chainsaws is no way to go through life! You will forget something that you can't afford to forget. I encourage you to do this daily, and you will become successful.

This also inspires confidence in the customer that his concerns are being addressed and gives you an opportunity to expand and deepen your relationship with the customer.

While interviewing new salespeople, I always would take in consideration how they were dressed and how they carried themselves. I would take the opportunity to look in the window of their car. These salespeople are more interested in sales than their car. Before you think I am way off-base, this is only 75% of the time. I also look for energetic and outgoing people for sales. It was just an incidental observation, and not a "dyed in the wool" fact.

One thing you have to actively remember is to make yourself "**get responsive**" if you are extroverted.

You know that it is typically hard for you to focus on the client if you are worried about other things, but it will come easier the more you focus on your responses to customer problems or inquiries.

I have never understood why people cannot get back to me rapidly! I have always said, "**Time kills deals**." You are in control of your response time. It is amazing that police departments, fast food restaurants, school fire drills, and fire stations monitor and quantify their reaction times, and yet we do not. When you respond quickly, your customer will then begin to feel important. When they begin to feel important to you, they begin to develop loyalty, and loyalty brings revenue to the table.

If you actively track tasks daily, you will gain more business. If you keep track of the moving parts, you will notice the positive effect with your customers. There are many devices to help you get more responsive. Most of my managers asked me what made me successful, and the answer is: **be responsive.** You will have a hard time staying organized also, but it is critical in this modern era.

The cellular phone has made it easier to connect with people instantly. Use this tool daily. It is amazing how many people do not. Can I ask you a question? Do you have two mobile phones or devices? Use one for personal use, and one for work. It makes it easier to know who is calling and gives you the information you need to make a split-second decision on how to respond.

My customer always calls on my work phone, and it's powered on 24/7. You always want to be available to them, because they are always calling about something they need. It will always give you an advantage against and above your competition. Many people hit the "ignore" button on their phone, sending the call directly to voicemail. We have to do a better job in the work world communicating across the board. All communication should be responsive. Most sales jobs put less emphasis on the personal touch; however, being personal will set you apart. Really talk to people. The majority of customers enjoy talking to personable people. In the same respect, time is finite. There is a very thin line between being responsive and when you start to bother your customer. You have to have value when you are calling or visiting your customer. You also need to discern when space is needed so that you may provide that instead, when required.

So how do you become truly responsive in today's world? There is no question you have all the tools at your disposal. Great salespeople are procrastinators. It sounds funny, but it seems to be a major fault shared by highly social and effective salespeople. We will always put social first and work second. When work becomes fun, it will take priority over the social aspect. It is amazing when we have a deadline, we hunker down and get it done. I will guarantee you, highly social people are the same everywhere. We all share the same traits, and we work very similar. You have to make being responsive your number one priority, bottom line.

The phone system in 2015 irritates me more than anything in today's world. So much time is wasted hitting numbers to speak with someone in customer service. I am not saying that I always need to talk to someone, but most of the time I do. I like that verbal stimulation, and I also know that the task is complete when a human confirms that it is complete. The corporate phone system is making the workforce less productive in America. We are too reliant on what they provide. Why can't we talk to people more quickly? We never want a customer holding more than two minutes. Once again, this is the common sense that is scarce today. I have pushed made-up extensions and found people to connect me to a customer service representative. I have never been rude, but I keep knocking on the door until someone answers. Always remember, be highly empathetic with your

customer. ***The greater response time, the higher your sales volume.***

The main question that you need to ask yourself is, how responsive have you been in the past? Can you be more responsive? Will you be more responsive? It is so easy for salespeople to put off today what they can do tomorrow. We all do it, but how do we become more responsive? There is a lot going on in everyone's life, but we must take steps toward our customers concerns.

Salespeople often hate to give bad news. We *all* hate bad news, but it will always be better than **no** news. Challenge yourself from this point to always get out in front of the bad news. It will keep you ahead of your competition. I am not saying you will enjoy giving it; just be responsive on the bad news.

Your customer, in the end, will appreciate the candor and honesty.

It is not easy to be responsive. When you get great at doing it, you will become a "Great Salesperson". This trait will set you apart from the competition. At the end of the day, you have to remember people like things completed. The more responsive you become, the more tasks you accomplish. Being responsive will make you a true resource, and that will have the power over your competition. We all need an advantage over our competitors, would you not agree?

Chapter 2
Be Interested,
not Interesting

Think about that statement for a moment. I'm a salesperson; you have tons of stories. Perhaps my client will want to hear one or two of them sometime. The more critical action you can perform is to be interested in what they have to say and/or what problem you might be able to solve for them. There will be plenty of time to amuse them when we have developed a rapport. To that concern, every book you have read says, ***"People buy from people they like."*** This is 100% true. The question then becomes, "How do you get people to like you?" Most salespeople want to talk about themselves or the product. They always want to talk first and listen second.

Your first job will be to get your customer to talk first. You can do this in many ways. **Bonding** is a key ingredient in the sales process.

Survey your surroundings first, and begin a conversation focused on them. If they are wearing apparel with a sports team on clothing you know about, start the conversation about that team. The key is to be **genuine**. Do not use a canned approach; they will see it a mile away. Start with *"Can I ask you a question?"* It is a simple method to get the person talking. Remember, people like talking about themselves. It is easy to believe the one thing that everyone is an expert on is... themselves! If you have to take notes, then you are not actively showing **interest**. Have you ever taken notes on your family? You need to treat everyone like a family member.

You have to really drop your guard and talk to people. You have to **leave people better than you find them.** Make the first 15 minutes of a sales call about the customer. Enjoy hearing their story. We all are connected in some way. I promise you will find out the connection if you ask questions.

It is interesting to hear a person's story. I assure you, there are some great ones out there. It is like a movie when people are talking. Try to be empathetic when they are speaking. You need to get involved during the telling of a story. You need to be asking questions to get this to work. Listen and ask questions like, **"Tell me more. Really?**

How did that happen? How did you find yourself doing this job?"

I will reiterate the fact you have to be engaged. If you do not have the time to be actively engaged, then do not go down this road. It is enjoyable talking to people who want to talk. If you are not **genuine,** then people will not open up. There are salespeople all the time whom you think are good listeners, but when you ask them a question about their customer, they cannot tell you what they said. You must be involved and be sincere about your involvement.

It is a challenge to see people who do not want to see a salesperson. There is no shortage of them! I had to make a call once on such a customer. Once, a colleague set me up (either as a joke or a challenge) to call on such a customer.

When I called Danny Wheeles, he was angry. He said that he would never buy anything from my company ever again. He said my company was filled with a **"bunch of liars."** Danny hung up on me. My colleague laughed. So I got in my car and drove to Danny's company. I asked to speak with him. He politely said," You have guts." So I then started asking questions as to figure out why he thought we were liars.

Apparently, we had lied to him over some part of the delivery. I promptly explained that I had not lied to him and would not lie to him. Then I noticed he had a small motorcycle on his desk. That little motorcycle started a conversation that went on for 20 minutes. When the time felt right,

I asked him to give us another chance. He was so involved with our conversation, he gave me an order.

At this point, it was important to pick up his order and take it back to his office. He said, "Is this the kind of service I can expect?" I said, "Yes." We have been friends now for 5 years.

Danny learned I cared more about him than his account. He knew I did not want to let him down as a friend. I was his guy. You want to be your customer's "go-to guy". In order to do this, you have to get personally invested to give true customer service. You want to see your customer and make sure that they are satisfied.

I have met thousands of people who are attached in some fashion. We all are connected in some way or another. This has to be a **"you thing"**. If you do not want to talk to other people, you are definitely in the wrong profession.

Most people are interesting. They want to tell you about everything that is important to them. If being interested can make you a better salesperson and a better person, would you do it?

When I am talking to a group, I try to explain the *"hear you"* will **"process the information"** and **"store it."**

That is to say, if you casually listen to someone, it will filter out, fall into the background noise. When your mother talks to you, most of the time you hear; when you just listen, some things you usually forget.

I have always wanted people in a seminar to hear. The problem is that the human brain can only focus so long on a particular thing. Have you ever noticed on TV why frames change every seven seconds? They are trying to keep you engaged. We are social animals and things change rapidly. You have to stay focused on your customers. The true rainmakers are genuine and always interested. The challenge is this: (1) get in the game; (2) be interested; and (3) be an active listener.

It will amaze you how this technique starts to work. The true sign of being interested is when you start telling the stories you have heard to other people.

The company for which I worked told me that I was a "name-dropper". If I had low self-esteem, I would have taken offense to that statement. You need to always make a conscious effort to meet as many people as you can. A person's life is measured by the good they do. More often than not, the "name-dropping" I was accused of was happening as a result of re-telling the personal stories of customers and leaving others better than I found them (including myself).

Salespeople are door openers, and if you have a true team, they can help you with any obstacle you have. We need to know ourselves. For example, I have learned that I am skilled at discovering people's strengths. That is how I came to be a trainer and motivator. Other administrators could recognize this talent and encouraged me to become a trainer.

Why is it we do not ask for help, discover where we are weakest, and determine in what areas we should be trained?

One reason we are not rainmakers is --
Fear! We are afraid that our value will
decrease with the company or colleagues.
Forget fear! It is not easy to do, but it
becomes easier with practice. Make a habit
of eliminating fear from your life.

True leaders have little fear of failure. It
is exactly why a successful manager   can
weather   tough   situations.   You   must
surround yourself with a team that is as
good as, or better than you.

This should be a compliment that your
tree has branched out. People's egos will get
in the way of their success. They are afraid
that the next salesperson is better than they
are and that as a result they will get fired.
This is not true.

The true **team** concept will only work if
you allow it to work. We stand in our own

way and hold ourselves back. How can you be responsive if you are worrying that your teammate is making you look bad? You must trust and verify. How can you share stories with your team if you are worried about the colleague being better? The one thing I ask is to go out and meet someone today. Hear their story and share it with someone. I promise you, it will make you a better person.

I was talking to a great salesperson named Ken Gerrard. He is a vice president of business development for an excellent company. He told me the second he returns from a visit with a potential client, his people want to know what projects they have and whom they are using. He explains to them he does not know yet. He has spent the last two hours being *interested*, not *interesting*. He is trying to learn about his future client. He is trying to hear what they are saying. Ken knows there is an art to timing, and he has done this long enough to know when the time is right to talk about his company and what they have to offer. He also explained to me not everyone in your organization will understand what you do, and that they do not need to. Ken said, "Our job is to drive revenue, and these positions are hard to fill; sales is a hard job. I believe you can learn a skill set, but to be a true master of those skills is a God given talent."

It is easy to talk about yourself, because it is the one subject in which you are an expert. Due to this, you have to remain vigilant and engaged with the customer. There will always be time to talk about you when the time is right. When you get to the end of the book, you will know when that time comes available. While observing salespeople, they are always waiting to talk about themselves instead of the customer. If you focus on only asking questions, it will make it difficult for you to talk about yourself. You must remember that it must be about the **customer,** not **you.**

This skill is maybe the toughest to master as sales professionals, because we love to talk. It is how we make our livings, yes? The great thing is, when you get their story, you can share it with someone else. We love to tell things about our life, and it is your job to get really good at learning people's stories.

We call a salesperson who cannot listen to someone *"a shows up and throws up".* They will tell you they are great at sales. My teams never told me they were great --- they showed me. If you are great, your results will speak for you.

The next part of this chapter is one of the most valuable tools in a salesperson's arsenal. The following formula is the reason great salespeople are great. All salespeople have three skill sets to be great. They have to have **job skills**, **sales skills,** and **personal skills**. You will note, the personal skills are the most important of the three. You will always get more accomplished by being well-liked. In the following equation you will see how important it becomes to have great personal skills. This formula is one reason why I believe I was successful in the sales field.

The equation goes like this:

$$A + B \times C = Y$$

A= Job Skills
B= Sales Skills
C= Personal Skills
Y= Sales Quotient

Job Skills + Sales Skills (Personal Skills) =Sales Quotient

Let's start with *job skills*. These are skills that have been learned about your job. They can be many things that you regularly practice: product knowledge, computer skills, and technical skills, anything that pertains to your job. You should evaluate yourself on a scale from **one** to **ten.**

The second variable is rating your *sales skills*. This measures how good a salesperson you are and how well you grade yourself in selling in the field or over the phone. These competencies also include closing skills, greeting skills, actively listening, features and benefits, etc., and the numbers you earn.

The last element in this equation measures your set of ***personal skills***. Some examples of personal skills would include conversation skills, active listening abilities, and how well you are able to bond with your customer. Personal skills are the most important of all the skills.

This exercise will explain just how critical your personal skills really are in relation to your success.

Let's say you are a nine on job skills and an eight on sales skills, but on personal skills you score a five. Your equation would look like this:

$$9 + 8 \times 5 = 85$$

Now let's say you are a six on job skills and six on sales skills, but a ten on your personal skills. Your equation would look like this:

$$6 + 6 \times 10 = 120$$

Your personal skills are the multiplier. No matter how skilled someone is at their job, if they have poor personal skills, they will never be a successful salesperson. It is for this reason that a team's personal skills always require the most work.

You may think of personal skills as software, and it needs the most work and the most tweaking. If you have a genuine interest in your customer, this skill will come to you much more easily. If you are interested in people, your personal skills will be higher. You begin to relate better to people better than your competition.

This formula is an eye-opener. It explains so much about the sales process. Remember to work on all skill sets in the overall equation, *but spend the most time on the development of your personal skills.* The good news is, the personal skills are the easiest to master. It takes less time to sharpen those skills than the job skills. The other two elements are important, but really work hard on the personal connection.

When managers are searching for "A" players in the hiring process, likability is the number one skill they are looking to find. If you are not well-liked, you are not doing your job. The onus falls on you if your customer does not like you. You have to be interested in others to be well-liked. It will be more difficult for your customer to say "no" to someone they actually like. If your new hire is not likable, then he or she will not reach their true potential. The more you listen, the more interested you will become. One way to remind yourself of this is to remember the 70/30 rule. **You must listen 70 % of the time and talk 30% of the time.** This will be one of the most difficult things in the sales process. It is natural to want to talk and add to stories. You must commit to listening. It will always help you close more business. This is a highly sought after skill set when hiring salespeople. If they are liked, they are highly regarded by other people. If you are liked, you will make people feel OK. Please do not think if you are liked, you will be successful in sales. It will help you be more successful. We all want to be liked in some sort of fashion. It makes things so much easier in life when people like you. You will start to close more business. **People buy from people they like**.

Chapter 3
"It's not about what it is about"

There was once a sign in my office that said, ***"It is not about what it is about."*** This quote has been a staple looming over visitors to my office and indicates how I have lived my life the last 20 years. The obvious problem is never the real problem. You have to peel back the layers of the onion and get to the real problem. It is a well known fact that angry people are easy to sell. They always tell you what you are doing wrong. Can you imagine going to the doctor and never telling him what your symptoms are? If you walked in and did not say a word, he could not treat you effectively. Take this one step further; could you imagine telling him the wrong symptoms and still hope he could cure you? Unfortunately, the same approach happens every day to salespeople. Your customer will quit buying from you and never tell you why. It is easy when a customer tells you that you have poor customer service skills, or you are too expensive. It is what is unsaid that we have a tough time understanding. That is exactly why you have to ask questions.

It is amazing how we end up discovering a problem that we never knew we had. You have to remember, what you do not know in sales will kill you. You have to get all the "negatives" out of the way. What are the objections? What are the true reasons they are not buying?

When people get angry, it is rarely about the true problem. There is always the "proverbial straw that breaks the camel's back". It is a multitude of problems. You have to ask the right questions to get the real answer. How many times have you thought one thing was the reason something happened, and then the real reason was actually totally different?

So how do you really find the truth in a sales situation?

You must drill down in an effective matter that your customer does not feel like they are being interrogated.

You must be **genuine** when asking questions. You also must remember you are asking questions to help the customer in a sales situation. If you are not really vested in finding out how you can help your customer, then you will never have a loyal customer. If you are not **genuine**, the customer will know, and they will leave you to go to the next salesperson.

You must also remember you are building a relationship that will last when someone else comes knocking at their door. There will always be another salesman right behind you, knocking on their door.

So when you hear, "**It is not about what it is about**", just what does that mean? If you have ever dealt with angry people, you know it is difficult. The first step is to move toward them. It is human nature to run away from problems or angry people. Moving towards them is going to be one of the toughest things to do, but you must commit to the situation. The person wants to be heard first and foremost. Allow customers to get all their issues out on the table. Listen actively, and do not make comments while they are expressing their anger. **Only ask questions.**

Once they are done (and you will know when they are finished), this simple statement will get you further than anything else you can do: "**Now, can I ask you a question? What would you like me to do?**"

Remember, you cannot be condescending in any way. Allow them to tell you what they think you should do. This does not mean that you will meet their demands; it means they are on the table. Once the emotion is out of the problem, we can determine what really can be done.

Ultimately, people just want to be heard. We just need to listen to them. They almost always calm down after they have expressed the problems out in the open. At this point, it is the most important task to keep the questions coming. You have to remember that you are asking questions to solve a problem or build value. You are the solution!

What you do not know in sales will *kill you*. This statement simply means that the **unknowns are the key to business**. You must ask questions to discover why they are going to buy from you or someone else. When people say, "**buyers are liars**", it can be uncomfortable; a better explanation would be "***buyers are 'tryers'***". They will test you to see how knowledgeable you are, or if you will come off the price.

There is nothing wrong with being tested, and if you are great at asking questions, you will never get caught up when they do test you. In order to get the true answer, you have to be genuine.

It's a paradigm shift, but it works seamlessly when you are great at it. For example, when a customer asks you, "Can you lower your price?" You say, "Is my price too high?" If they say yes, you say, "Compared to?" This will tell you whom you are competing against. You may have to drill down further, but you get my point. It works so easy if you just ask. That one or two word question has just given you the competitor. It is that simple.

"Can you deliver tomorrow?" Your response: "Do you need it tomorrow? Can you wait until the next day?" You now have their delivery schedule.

If they ask, "Do you have it in stock? Can I call and see? If I do, will you place an order today?" Once again, this is a thin line you are walking, and if you are not genuine, then they will get tired very quickly of being interrogated.

These are surface questions a customer will ask because they have been trained to ask them. What you are trying to do is discover what it is they truly want. This is an art form that anyone can master. There is nothing dishonest or underhanded about finding out the real reason that they are asking a question. This is called getting *"the why behind the what"*. Discovering this information will help you build a tremendous value. If you know your customer buys based on price rather than service, why would you not want to know that?

You may not be the cheapest, so why not get that out in the open? People who buy on price do not understand value.

I never buy the cheapest gas in town, unless there is not a line. Wouldn't you rather pay more not to deal with a crowd? What you have to understand is, I understand value. My time is more valuable than $2.00. My car holds about 31 gallons, and $.06 relates to about $1.86. We are trained that the billboard is the "say all - be all." A person who buys gas usually goes inside and pays more for a drink than they save in gas. We are taught to buy gas cheaply because it's a commodity. I understand it's tough not to want to save money, but is there value in it? What is your time worth?

In the grand scheme of things, it's not about the price; it's that you feel confident you are getting a good deal because the masses are here.

Why is cheapest a great deal? If you got in an accident while waiting in a crowd, would it have value? I understand people can justify anything, but the value of gas is too minimal for me to get in a huge line.

My point is simple: it's not about me saving $.06 a gallon. The main reason is, the employees know me, and I know I can get in and out at a certain time, and they make me feel **OK.** We are creatures of habit, and we like what is easy. So it may be about making the buying easy for your customer. Customers have shared that they buy from a competitor because it is easy.

There is a story about a man buying a bone-in-ham for his wife. When the man left to go to the butcher, he was told by his wife to cut the end off. He knew to cut the end off, because they had always cut the end off. However, this time he wanted to get **"the why"** behind **"the what".**

He called his wife to ask why they cut off the end of the ham. She said, "Because Mom always did." The man then called his mother-in-law and asked the same question. She said because her mother did the same. He was fortunate to have his wife's grandmother living, so he called her and asked the same question. She replied, "My five quart pan is only so big, so the ham would not fit unless I cut the end off."

The point to all this is that we figure out why we are doing things, and there may be a

49

better way. Never take things at face value. The more questions you ask, the more knowledgeable you will become. There is nothing wrong with conformity, but when it comes to selling, you want to be different.

You always want to be remembered by your customers. You want customers to think of you when they need something. The truth is, everyone feels so much better when they are helping people.

We have to get great at asking questions. The questions help us understand the customer and the real reason they are buying. We need to keep drilling down for the right reason.

My father always told me that people hate the truth. The truth is a metric that holds people accountable. Why do we dislike the truth? The reason is simple: it gives us accountability. It is your job to find out why people are buying from your competition. The sales process will stall if you let it, because people do not want to tell you the truth. You have to let them feel **"OK"** to get the real reason why they are not buying from you. In most of the cases, people just do not like telling you "no". If you really are liked, it makes it even harder.

Emotion is a huge factor in the sales process. It is a key component of the saying "It is not about what it is about". You have to take emotion out of the sales process. It is incredibly frustrating to lose a deal and be unclear of the reason why it was lost. One way to improve upon this is to start reviewing deals together as a team and talk about what was said. We figured it out; it was called "watching film". Salespeople are very emotional people. The great ones know how to channel emotion into behaviors. It will always be difficult to do this, but you have to remain committed to the process. I am guilty of this more than anyone. You have to keep your negative emotions always in check. We call this in the sales process **"close to the vest".** It is always okay to be emotional, but it really depends on who observes your emotions.

An example of emotional behavior is a story when I worked for a large builder in the Carolinas. I had an administrative assistant that I truly loved. She and I became really great friends because of loyalty and a true working relationship. She had a very detailed personality, and it complimented my social personality well. The first day we worked together, she came in at 8:05 AM. I explained to Irene that she was late. This was early in my management career. She did not feel **"OK"**. "She explained to me that if she left her home any earlier that the traffic would be worse, which is why she leaves work at 5:15 PM. I observed her for 4 years do exactly what she explained. Irene would get to work every morning at the same time. She had the exact same morning routine. She would sit at her desk, get her coffee cup, and bring her spoon with her. Irene would wash the spoon and sit back at her desk. She then would pull out her hair brush and stroke each side three times. After that, she would then put on her lipstick, and then begin work. It was exactly 8:15 AM when this daily ritual was complete... so why do you think I am telling you Irene Stone's habits? It was the first time I was taught not to take things at face value. She was one of the best co-workers I have had in my entire career. She taught me the value of details, and she also protected me from my bosses. When I was emotional, she was the witness and helped me to be less emotional and to control myself. We made a great team together. A detailed ally like Irene can be an invaluable asset to you in the sales world.

People tend to be emotional when they undergo the home buying process. It is one of the largest investments people make in their lifetime. When people get angry, it is not usually over trivial things like the sink being two inches off their preference. It is always about something else. In some strange way, you become a pseudo-psychiatrist for your customer through the duration of the sale. In a unique way, I discovered you have to make people feel OK.

Never take things at face value. In order to do this, you must remember to get the details and drill down to find the real answer. If you apply this not only to sales, but also in life, you will start to gain an understanding why people do the things they do. Most of the time, you'll see that "it is not about what it is about."

Chapter 4
Fear

When conducting a sales seminar, I always ask the audience, "Who is the best salesperson that you know?" Generally, a few people say, "Me," and then some name another person. The second question I ask is, "Who has children?" There are always people in the room who have kids. The best salespeople we know are children. They can convince Mom and Dad almost every time.

Why? Simple: they have no fear. They are not afraid of being told "no." It does not hurt to ask, and most of the time we say, "Yes." Children do not have the years of rejection that parents have. They also have a better leverage on getting a "yes" response.

Fifteen years ago, I discovered that fear stops us from doing two things: fear stops us from being successful, and fear stops us from being that which we truly are.

If you can control fear, you can do anything you want. Unlike children, salespeople have a fear of being told "no." How do you control fear? Here is the easy part. It is simple: you just get it out on the table. **When you tell your customer about your fear, your *fear* goes away.**

Here is an example. If you have a fear, the customer will not buy from you. Try this: **Can I ask you a question?** "My fear is that you like my price, but you won't buy from me; is that a fair question?"

They will then tell you what you need to know. My biggest fear was they would shop my quote around when I left. So, I would say, "If I give you a price that will keep you from shopping, would that save you some time?" If he says, "Yes," ask, "What would that price be?" Your customer has just given you their budget parameters. You have the opportunity to meet or decline the price. This stuff is simple. When you take away your fear, the close will follow. It will give you a clear direction on what your customer is thinking. If you think your price is too high, just say it. "My fear is you will think my price is too high." It will give your customer an out. It will also tell you if your quoted price is too high.

Do not be afraid of anything in the sales process. If you are, then just put it on the table. It is a true relief when you do not have to worry about what you are not covering.

You need to be genuine, honest, and transparent.

The statement you want to remember is "My biggest fear is _____." This will give you a high point of leverage. You will always end up fearing stuff that does not matter. Is it not amazing nothing is as bad as we make it out to be! Salespeople hate to go in a cold call situation, either on the phone or at a place of business. Let us remove fear from the equation.

Tell your customer that your biggest fear is that you are not going to be able to feel comfortable introducing yourself. The customer will not let you struggle. It is human nature not to want to see someone struggle. Everyone is ready to help. It is not uncommon to find a salesperson prepping outside their meeting place to feel ready and comfortable. "What are you preparing for?" You have no idea what is going to happen when you walk in the door. You are a door opener.

The most important thing is what to do when you open the door. Salespeople believe they can sell everyone. This is a misconception. The truth of the matter is, not everyone is your customer. Here is a simple way to get around that fact.

"My biggest fear is when we are done talking about my company, we may not be a fit. I am afraid you will not tell me, is that a fair statement?" You have taken the pressure off the customer to say "no" to you. A "no" is just as important as a "yes." It releases you from wasting the customer's time. You have to make the customer feel **"OK"**, whatever they tell you.

Imagine you or your sales team never allowing fear to stop them ever again. Do not be afraid to say it; just get the fear out there. You must take the emotion out of the process. When fear is gone, the process is much simpler. If you have a fear, state it.

When you become great at asking questions, your fears will diminish greatly. You can never be afraid you are asking the tough questions. This becomes very easy to do, the more you do it.

When I was selling homes, I always asked the customer, "My biggest fear is when you get home, you will have buyer's remorse. Is that a fair question?" I put it out there on the table. Why is it so difficult for us to state the obvious? I promise you will handle a ton of objections up front. Most salespeople do not want to state the obvious because they are afraid they will lose the sale. I remember when we were at the closing table. I always explained to the customer that the contract they were signing was prepared by the company and all 23 pages were to protect us. I explained if you were going to use us as a builder, then you must sign our contract. The sales staff hated me saying that. We never lost one customer over making that statement. They were so excited about buying a home, and no one else ever told them that. It was the obvious.

Our attorneys had prepared the paperwork, and they worked for us. I also told them they had three days to rescind the offer. They should go home and read all the documents.

If we lost the sale, it was because of some other reason. We had no fear that the contract would cost us a sale. We also knew every purchase contract was the same. It is amazing when we buy a car that all the paperwork is prepared by the seller and to protect them. The seller will not state those facts ever in the closing.

When we apply for a credit card, you rarely read all the terms and conditions. You normally just look at the rate. It is understood even still that if we are going to use their money, you must abide by their rules. Interesting enough, people still do not care very much. When you make a payment on your American Express account, you just click the box indicating you agree to the terms and conditions. You do this because you see the value in doing business with the company. Should we not be more concerned once we know the importance of what we are signing? We have been trained that if we want to buy, we must follow the conditions of buying.

So, how do you get rid of fear? The acronym for fear is:

FEAR
Forgetting
Everything
About
Reality

When we have anxiety, it is usually about everything *except* reality. Our mind takes over, and we forget that it is never as bad as we expect. You must stay in the present moment and deal with it before moving to the next thing.

When I was a teenager, I was afraid of snakes. I purchased a python and became a snake owner. It was truly difficult for me to handle the snake at first. I knew I had to force myself to get over my fear. The confidence I felt after handling the snake for a month was incredible. I was truly proud of myself for overcoming something that gave me so much anxiety.

It is a fact that the customer will not bite you. We have to get comfortable dealing with our fears in the workplace. You will be truly amazed what you can accomplish when fear is not present in your life. Challenge yourself today! If you have a fear, state it and overcome the anxiety of that fear. Facing that fear will take the power away from it, offering you a non-obstructed pathway toward success.

You should never have any fear about anything in the sales process. You will never have all the answers, but you can always make sure you know someone who does.

Go ahead and write down their question, and come back to it when you have your resource available to provide the correct answer. It is a simple skill you will become great at when you lose the fear that you may not immediately know all the right answers for the customer.

Fear is a fact of life, but you should never have a fear in talking with a customer. Occasionally, in meetings, customers will try to push you to answers you do not have at your fingertips; just do not panic, and come back to it when you have the right answer.

You should challenge yourself to talk with your colleagues about parts in the sales process you are uncomfortable with. As a team, address those until you feel comfortable dealing with them. There are some salespeople who feel uncomfortable when they meet new people. It should be easily overcome if you keep the conversation focused on the customer; they will make you feel "**OK**" if you talk more about them than yourself, or the product.

This will not be profound or religious, but pure, stated fact. We are all dying, and one day it will be all over. We all have fear, and how we handle it is different. I hope you never let it stand in your way, as I have done in my life. It is one thing we all have in common. So why talk about death in a sales book? Simple: it is the ultimate unknown. You need to know that your time is limited, and you need to stop aiming low and hitting instead at aiming high and missing. You may disagree with some of the things you have read in the first few chapters. Then I encourage you to follow your steps to be successful and use only what you need, that will truly be fearless. You need to have the courage to put yourself out there and ask questions.

Most salespeople are afraid to get outside the box. We all fear rejection, but you must embrace it. The reason most people give up is because they do not see instant results. The one thing you know is that this is a numbers game. You must ask many questions to get to the real reason. The mindset will need to be in place, and you cannot have fear in pushing along until you get the real reason the customer wants to buy from you. You will discover fear is an excuse for the weak not to achieve. There is a saying: ***"Audaces Fortuna iuvat--***

(Latin)--Fortune favors the bold. You will have to be bold to keep asking questions and changing your sales techniques.

My goal for any salesperson is to be the best you can be and keep trying to sharpen your skill set. We all can improve who we are as a person and colleague. If something is not working, be bold and fearless enough to change. Never be afraid of change; it is the cycle of life. You can always reinvent your sales techniques using the same fundamentals this book explains. You must stay the course but be willing to find what works for that given customer. If you keep asking questions, you will find the right answer.

Let's talk about how fear works outside the sales arena. Fear will always be a part of your life. The great news is, that you can control it. If you allow your fear to be more powerful than you are, then it will begin to define you. It will make your decisions for you. We all face fear in one form or another, and how we handle it makes us who we are. The first time I spoke in front of an audience, I had fear. The moment someone laughed at a joke, the fear subsided and I pushed through the presentation. When you are prepared, there will be very little fear. We all do not know what the future holds, but we start every day like the day before. It will be amazing what you can accomplish when fear is not present in your life. I promise you, your greatest success will come from facing your fear. Fear is self-imposed. We all create it, and we all can destroy it. For the betterment of your life and your career in sales, take the time to face your fears. It will lead to many successes in your life.

Chapter 5
Certainty

I never understood all the components that made me truly successful in the sales profession until I went to a sales seminar. The speaker told us we had to be certain we were in the right field. I asked myself on the ride home what he meant. I was always certain I was doing what I wanted and was skilled at the job. What resonated with me was how you obtained that feeling of confidence and how you could be sure to utilize that confidence to the fullest extent. You have to be in the "state of certainty". It is very much akin to when you need to make a putt---you have to know you are going to make it. Alternatively, when people miss a putt, it is usually because they tried to "wish it in." When you are in the state of certainty, you know you are going to make something happen. When two people meet, the most certain or confident will always have the most influence.

Certainty^2> Influence

You need to keep your body language at the same state as your confidence level. This process should be imperceptible to the client or the competition.

Like many sales trainers always say, **Fake it until you make it**. Your shoulders need to be up, and your chest out. There is a very thin line of being overconfident, but it is a skill that you must hone to a fine edge. If you confront someone who is in this feeling of certainty, you can mimic his or her posture and body language. Be sure that your perception of your demeanor is not of overconfidence or arrogance. The goal here is to appear certain.

Understand that when two people argue, the one who is most certain and sure of his argument can convince the other of anything. This can be achieved by believing in what you have to say. It is also known as positive thinking. I don't believe you can wish anything to happen. You must take action. It starts with your behavior. The old saying is, ***"If wishes were horses, beggars would ride."*** You must do the work.

The small things you do every day make up your actions. If you start your day with the proper techniques, you will have proper actions. This will then turn into results. Follow the formula based on personal skills.

These three items will always put you in the feeling of certainty. Repetition of this formula will give you this feeling. The more time you are in this state, it will become second nature. It is one reason great athletes perform in tight situations. They have been there many times, and it takes over on its own. They are completely prepared and certain of their preparation.

When you are doing the work, you will be ready when the time approaches. We as salespeople should be prepared and recognize when those moments come in the presentation. **"Most pro athletes call this the grind."** It is putting in the work to become a high performer. There are no shortcuts to success. You have to be willing to grind.

These components can be spelled out thusly:

BAR
Behavior – belief and practice
Actions – practice for success
Results – visualize success

When you look at top athletes, you know they will respond in a certain way because they have done the behaviors that lead to actions that lead to results. They get in a state of certainty or get in the zone. This is a better term than confidence. There are people who are confident but do not get results. I think people call this overconfidence. It is hard to explain, but when you are in the state of certainty, the clarity is unreal. You know how things are going to end.

I ask people in my seminars where they are the most comfortable or secure. I get a ton of responses, from their home to work, church, and a police station. The responses I receive are incredibly interesting. Once they have identified their preference, I ask them to rate their level of comfort on a scale of one to ten.

They always say, "Ten." I then instruct them to multiply their answer by 1000. This is how I feel on the golf course. For example, I hit about 80% of the fairways off the tee. My friends say CNN cuts to breaking news on TV when I miss a fairway. It is simple; when I hit my tee ball, I am in the state of certainty. I know I am going to hit it on the fairway. I have done the behaviors that cause the actions that will give me results. You have to enjoy sales like a game.

You have to have a passion to do the fundamentals. I often say, **"Sales training is like bathing: if you do not do it daily, you will stink."** Before Tom Brady or Peyton Manning get on the field, they are taking snaps and throwing short passes. They are getting in the zone. They are doing the behaviors to yield results. The coaches call this muscle memory. When you get really good at asking questions, it will feel like being in the zone. When you are genuine and really interested in the customer, the questions will be fluid.

There is no manipulation here; you are in a discovery mode with the goal to help your customer. This will start just like breathing, because you are truly trying to help them solve their problems. Once you become a pro at this, the relationship building will fall in place. The customer can really tell you are interested and will start to share things that he is not doing with your competitor.

They will be able to trust you as their *"go to guy or girl"*. This relationship will grow, and you will have to feed it. Be genuine, have that feeling of certainty, truly care for your customer's needs over your own- without manipulation or ulterior motives. It has been said that nothing happens until someone sells something. Most people call it consulting. I like to call it selling. If you are great at what you do, where is the shame? We call it sales, but sales is really like being a detective and trying to find the answers to help you close more business.

Look at show clips of Peter Falk in the series of *Columbo* to see how these answers can turn on the simplest questions.

You can see that even if you know the answer, letting the customer tell you what you need to hear will lay the answers open for everyone to see. When customers solve their own objections, they never resurface, and you have become their partner and go-to person. I know Columbo was always in the feeling of certainty. He was confident of the questions he was asking because he knew the answers. When I worked for the owner of a large company, he would always ask you a question to which he knew the answer. He wanted to see your response. If you got the question right, he would ask you how you arrived at the answer. It always made me feel like I was in geometry class and I had to show my work. He was always certain he was right. He was so certain he could influence your answer. I never felt OK when I was talking to him. He thought that would give him an upper hand. I never wanted my team to feel intimidated by my questions. If you were fearful of the right answer, then maybe you would hold back. This was a clear power struggle, and because of the way he dealt with all his employees, I did not look forward to hearing from him.

Can you imagine not ever wanting to talk to a leader? I was not the only one who felt this way; the whole company did. You can learn many things from people, even though they are not helping you. I did take away one thing that I will never forget. He explained there were two types of people in life: **"Those who go through life, and those who go through life and pay attention."**

I have never forgotten those words, and I make sure I pay attention. It was the only thing I got out of a five-year employment where the owner never made you **"OK"**. You never want to be patronized, but you want to be respected.

If you are currently in a situation where you feel undervalued at your workplace, then you should be looking for a better work environment. The principles in this book will hone your skills and be infinitely more marketable to future employers. When you are in the feeling of certainty, you will know that other companies are looking for great salespeople. You are a valued commodity! I know I have always been searching for great salespeople. You have to remember, nothing happens until someone sells something. These skills will help you feel certain that you have tremendous value in the workforce. Continue working to break through your fears, and they will no longer hold you back. The customer will appreciate what you are saying and give you the answers you need. You just have to remember to keep asking questions. If you are in a total feeling of certainty, you will know exactly where you are going to end up in the sales process. It will be a tremendous feeling, and you will possess it. The great news is that certainty is self-imposed. It will be controlled by you. Make the decision, and do the behaviors and the actions; the results will always follow. The most certain you are in life, the most influence you will have.

All great leaders have a tremendous influence. When they stop having influence, then they stop leading. Challenge yourself to find this feeling! It will influence everyone on your team. The fundamentals of selling are always in your control.

Chapter 6
Be Genuine

This chapter covers one of the most difficult pieces of the puzzle for most salespeople to grasp. They always get tripped up on being *genuine*. If you have a personality that is analytical, you have to learn to be less introverted, so the question becomes, if I'm putting that on, how am I being genuine? This is simple, if practiced; just be honest. You need to tell your customer that you are analytical, and I may miss something that is important, but with his or her help, you will be less likely to miss something important. "Can you help me with that?" People are inclined to help. This reverts back to fear. If you get your fear on the table, you are being genuine. Most analytical people want to have all the answers, and you want your customer to have all the answers. If you are always asking questions and not making statements, then this becomes problematic. Your team may need to help you, but you may also need help with the details. You must make this a team effort.

One great quote about working as a team is,

"If you give your team permission to fail, they will always tell you the truth."

How profound a statement this really is! There is never a reason to lie. If you are truly genuine, then there is only trust. My wife and I have always had an open relationship with our children. They have always had permission to fail. There have been many times that we wouldn't have caught a problem if they had not come to me first. Because of trust they had in us, and the trust we had in them, they have always been truthful.

It is hard for a parent to fulfill the many duties that make up the role of a parent. You never want to see your children struggle, and even still, you want them to know that you are always there to help. Coincidentally, this philosophy also worked with my sales team. Building a relationship with my team gave them the total autonomy they needed to make their own decisions. It is unbelievable the amount of growth a person can go through when they know you genuinely care about their well-being. You cannot be successful if your team is not. You can win some battles, but you cannot win the war.

Personally, I have always taken an interest in the family and friends of my sales team. Because of this, it is easy to discern when something is not right. The most successful people have their family lives in order in other areas. They understand that to be successful, they must achieve balance.

If you watch any sporting event, when they win, the first shot is a picture of the family. When someone wins a golf tournament, the children come out to celebrate. It takes everyone to be successful in a work environment, and no one segment is more important than the family. When you look at the greatest companies in today's world, *balance* is the key. They truly get it. We are not trained to be slave drivers, though working hard is the key to success. No one is capable of reaching the top without some help.

People always ask, "How can you care about someone you just met"? This quality is internal. You must let your guard down and get involved with the person. The main reason I like to hear a person's story is because we all are connected in some way. We are connected at a major level. We all are human beings. The next thing is up to you. If you listen to them for fifteen minutes, you will have a promising start of a personal connection. Personal connections are where all long lasting relationships begin.

It is difficult for salespeople to actively *listen* or *hear*. You must channel your emotion elsewhere when you feel compelled to interrupt or add to a story. This is the thin line I mentioned before, and the truly great salespeople know how to walk it well.

Salespeople always wish to jump in and tell you how their experience relates to yours. These people are referred to as **"one-uppers".** It does not matter how great the story is being told; their contribution to the story is better. Keep in mind, you are the director, and you have to let the story develop organically. The more you let the customer feel *"OK"*, they will share everything.

During a sales seminar, Walter Bond shared, **"The best-kept secret in business today is the likeability factor."** He says it does not matter what that resume says and that the background communicates.

In the sales industry, you must hire a person that is likeable.

You will always sell more when people like you. If a manager is well-liked by their team, they will work harder for him or her. Alternatively, some people love to be disliked. They believe they must garner respect. Instead, they should concentrate on being firm but fair. Kindness is not weakness.

My uncle Bill Rogers was a news anchor for 30 years. He always said *kindness* is the cheapest thing you can give someone. The bosses I liked the most were kind and focused. I inadvertently worked the hardest for people I liked. I never wanted to disappoint them. I have had managers tell me if they are nice to salespeople, they will walk all over them. This is 100% wrong. If you set the proper expectations and lead from the front, your salespeople will not walk over you. You both show up to work each day to provide for your family, and if either of you are not meeting the agreed upon expectations, then it is time to have a talk. You must never let salespeople drag you into emotion. You always have to remain professional.

Another critical aspect of the sales process is, **"How do you make a customer feel OK?"** The answer is, you start asking personal questions and actively listen to what they are saying. You are on offense, and they are on the defense.

Customers are trained and believe that salespeople are shady and not to be trusted. When you go on a sales call, you need to establish many things before you can get down to truly selling. The great salespeople know you have to be *genuine* and really there to help the customer. You always need to be truthful, even if your product or company may not be the best fit. Some people claim they can sell to everyone, but not everyone is a customer. You cannot have an ego in this business. You can always be certain, but not an egotist. People who are genuine do not have to be an egotist. They find their value in life does not depend on making a sale.

If you recall all great relationships you have had, the one thing in common with each of them was that each person was genuine with you. This does not mean they are always **genuine** with everyone, but with you they were.

It is a common belief that salespeople will try to be someone they are not. Some salespeople are trying to reinvent themselves, and in the process of doing so they truly forget who they are. If you become desensitized to understanding people and their personalities, you need more personal training. You do not necessarily need to be everyone's friend, because customers can see right through that. **You have to be genuine**. It makes sales so much more fun when you call on customers you like and they like you. It is your job to know when they do not like you. The likability factor is king. It will make the hard questions easy when you have done your job correctly. So what happens when the customer doesn't like you?

When you start to feel uneasy, we use a **T-O**, or a **"turn over"**.

You cannot have an ego. You must be able to let go and give the customer to someone else who can get further down the sales process with him or her. This happens often, and you can generally split the revenue with your colleague for making a reference. There is no room for ego when it comes to closing business. It is very simple: if you want to win more than you lose, you need the support of the team.

You will not sell everyone. You must recognize when you have stalled in the process. I always want a postmortem with my meetings with salespeople. It will be useful to see if they noticed something that you did not. We called it game planning or strategizing. Do not misinterpret being genuine as trying to gain acceptance by every customer. When you see a salesperson trying to be every customer's friend, the salesperson's margins are always quite low.

You have to build value, and being a great resource is valuable.

Make a challenge to yourself to be accountable, to not have an ego, and truly be genuine with your customers.

If you give people the permission to fail, they will always tell you the truth.

Oftentimes, we learn from failing. It reminds us the next time not to go down that same road. A great deal of experience is gained from failure. We have to get right back on the horse and move forward. It's very hard to hit a moving target, and you need to keep asking questions to help with a customer. You will learn more from failure than you will learn from successes.

It is not the successes in life that show you who you are; rather, it is the failures. It's not all the *"good stuff"* that shows you what life is about. Your strengths are forged in the weak places and tests we all encounter throughout life.

We have to have scars to remind us where we have been. It is at our lowest point when we learn how to be resilient.

You will always remember the ones you lost more than the ones you won. It is critical that you learn from your mistakes and know you will always get another chance to do a better job.

People will not only follow you just in sunshine, but when you go through tough times and become better as well. You need to understand all the emotions to become a great salesperson. You need to be able to relate to everyone in life. You have to be easy to relate to. You want everyone to feel *"OK"*. It is your job as a human being to make sure people always feel *"**OK**"*. You want to leave people better than you found them. How can you help them if you do not know why they are there?

These principles are easy to learn, and easier to master. Your closing ratio will go through the roof if people like you and you have value. You can build a tremendous amount of value by simply being genuine with your customers. You must be committed and buy in to this skill set. You cannot fake being genuine. It will be seen from miles away. However, if you are interested in others and not trying to appear interesting, then you will automatically be perceived by others as a genuine person. The secret is, one can't exist without the other. You now can see the dots starting to connect on how to become a great salesperson. When you become a great salesperson, you will also become a better person. You must always be genuine.

Chapter 7
Role vs. Identity

Role and identity are vitally important components in your self-development.

As you gain a broader understanding of who you are, what grounds you, and the various "hats" you will wear throughout your life - you will become more self-aware. Many of the other chapters in this book discuss the actual skill sets required to master the sales process. This chapter, alternatively, will discuss how to become a better you.

My friend Howard Stevens and I have had so many deep discussions about this topic. Howard was one of the smallest players in the National Football League. He played professional football for the New Orleans Saints and the Baltimore Colts.

Ironically enough, I did not meet Howard on the gridiron; I met him on the driving range. We were both hitting balls, and he migrated toward me. I initiated the conversation, and we talked for 30 minutes. The next day we played golf, and we have been true friends ever since. We laugh so much together that our stomachs hurt. It is amazing how much in common we have with each other.

I grew up idolizing pro athletes, and I recognized Howard from collecting football cards. My father owned a supermarket, and my brother and I used our money to collect cards. The moment I met him, I went back to my collection and sought out his card. I called my brother and told him about

Howard, and he remembered his card. We never knew Howard, but the card validated him. What is unique about Howard is he is genuinely interested in people. This was an important lesson taught by his family, to leave people better than you find them.

Howard also has a competitive spirit. No matter what he aspires to do, he brings that vitality. He is the kind of person who never gives up or gives in to anything. When people tell Howard that he is unable to accomplish something, Howard is the kind of man that sets out to prove them horribly wrong.

Howard also happens to be a scratch golfer and a remarkable pool player. One day during a round of golf, I was discussing my theory about identity with Howard. The funny thing was, he was way ahead of me because of his education as a psychology major at the University of Louisville. He let me finish the entire conversation and waited until the end to confess that he already knew all that I had shared with him. That was the moment I learned of how great a sales guy Howard was. He listened to me in order to be interested in the conversation; he had every right to pipe in to prove that he was more interesting than my story.

We all have roles we play. We are parents and grandparents. We are brothers and sisters. We are aunts and uncles. We are co-workers and bosses. The list goes on forever and ever. In most of my seminars, a question is presented to the attendees: on a scale of one to ten, score yourself in any given role. Most people give themselves an eight. Occasionally, people will give themselves a three or four. Next, they are asked:

"If you were on a deserted island, like Tom Hanks in the movie *Castaway,* with no one around and no roles to serve, what score would you give yourself?" Under this new premise, most people will score themselves one or two less than the original number.

The thing is, if you are an eight as a father, you are also an eight on the island. The island person is your true identity, and it must be the same as your role numeral. We all know people who, if they lose their job, will be distraught. Their role (or roles) defines who they are as a person. They cannot separate who they are from what they do for a living. We call this a "**low I**". They have a tremendous ego, and it is imperative to their worthiness as a person to establish value. "**Low I**"s believe if you show kindness, you are weak. This is far from the truth. Alternatively, when you have a **"high I"**, you are comfortable in your own skin.

"**Low I**"s are always trying to "one-up" you to make themselves look better than they are in reality. They are afraid to fail, because they fear people will look at them differently.

I once asked Howard how he made it in the NFL. He responded by telling me he did not have a choice. He said, *"Rick, do you know how many people told me I could not make it? Too many to count."* Howard has a **"high I"**. He is a 'ten" in everything he does in life. He always thinks he can accomplish everything he does... so he does! Often, he will try to bait me to take a bet on the premise he cannot do something.

However, I know Howard well enough to know that no matter the subject matter, I would always be on the losing end of that bet, so I never bite.

People who have **"high I"s** are always interested in others. They want to learn how to get better. They listen to people around them. When you become comfortable with your identity, you can do any role you set your mind to accomplish.

Many great salespeople are pretty much unorganized. While this is not always true, the great ones have to work on staying organized diligently. A person who has a **"high I"** likes the unplanned and the unknown. The people who have confusion in the **I & R** like things to be planned, predictable, and organized.

The person with a **"low I"** likes to be in control. Great sales people are fine with being called out in front of a crowd. In fact, they thrive on it! They love the spontaneity and attention.

Great salespeople can fake it. I always tell my sales team to **"Fake it until you make it!"** To be great in sales, you have to be able to call an audible at the line of scrimmage (and it takes guts!). You need to be able to roll with the punches. The military teaches you to overcome and adapt. U.S. Navy SEALS undoubtedly have **"high I"s.** If plan A is not working, you have to be willing to change to plan B. If you're still not seeing results, then there are 25 more letters to exhaust in the alphabet.

In summation, you must be comfortable with who you are and continue to grow with your personal development. This is vital in the sales industry.

People mostly manage how they were managed. This premise can cause some obstacles if your manager had a **"low I"**. You must let go of your fear and understand that your role is not your identity. A person with a **"low I"** is more likely to use phrases like "I, me, mine". They feel they have to tell you how important they are.

A person with a **"high I"** is more likely to use phrases like "we, our, us". It is truly about other people when you meet people with a **"high I".** The roles you play in life make up who you are as a person. When you put people first, you will always make them feel *"OK"*. This is the overarching mentality of a person who has a **"high I"**.

Seeing people succeed in life and grow in confidence is one of life's greatest joys. Most people with a **"low I"** have a false sense of confidence. They want to hide the fact that they are in the feeling of uncertainty, and they make more statements than ask questions. They want to make it about them. This is especially prevalent in management. They believe if they make it more about the team, they have no value. We all have value, but in different areas.

You must be able to give yourself permission to fail. Most people have been taught that if they fail, their value decreases. This is an internal lie. Instead, we must help people and not let them struggle. The dilemma with most people who have **"low I"s** is that they feel it will weaken them as a boss or a co-worker if they reach out to help another. This is truly not the case. It always has to be team first. This will become a coachable moment. Help your team in their growth and development by leaving them better than how you found them. That is the true mark of a great leader.

"We grow if we are green, and we rot if we are ripe." We always want to be growing in our careers and in life. It is fine that we do not know all the answers. Keep building a firm foundation for your identity; it's always a rewarding experience when we learn more about ourselves.

When you have a **"high I"** mentally, you can teach others around you to have one also. You can see a **"low I"** a mile away. Success breeds success. Brian Tracy says that your income will be the average of your five closest friends. Surround yourself with successful people. If you are in high school and you have a low GPA, then it is time to get some new friends. If your friends are always in trouble, migrate away from them. You have to be with people who have the same or higher goals and aspirations. It will also push them to meet their goals.

It doesn't have to always be about money. Successful teams usually carry themselves in a different matter. They know what it takes to be happy. It all starts with you. Successful people have a **"high I"** and are in the pursuit of happiness, even if they have not found it yet.

To be successful in life, you have to believe in yourself when no one else does. Avoid any mentor that is not a positive person. Negative people can drag you down. You cannot have a low self-esteem and be a true leader. If you do not believe in yourself, how will others believe in you? You must be certain that you will succeed, and your certainty will rub off on your team. Remember the old saying about a rising tide? The tide floats all boats! Commit to be that tide for your team.

When I look back at my career, the majority of conflict in management came from people with **"low I"s.** They felt the need to build themselves up when measuring against their peers. People who have **"low I"s** are caught up in what is called "**The CRAB PRINCIPLE**". Put simply, if you are succeeding, this principle indicates the natural propensity for people below you to drag you down. The origin of this saying comes from a natural phenomenon. When a crab is placed in a bucket alone, it tries to get out. But the moment you drop another crab in the bucket, he will drag any other crab down. The crab principle is evidence that the old saying is true, "misery loves company."

The main problem with people having a "**low I**" is that their metrics of success are off. "**Low I**" folks measure their shortcomings in a very real and tangible way. Alternatively, "**high I**"s want people to succeed. They know if someone gets "out of the bucket", they may pull them out also.

We are not measured by other people's standards; we are measured by our own standard. Golf is the same, because the game is built to weigh your own capabilities against the standard of the golf course and your own personal performance, instead of comparing yourself against another player.

People's failures or successes only have a bearing on us if we allow them to have an impact. We can learn from them, but they only need to be a metric for each individual.

Make your own goals in life, and remember that only your measurement of success is applicable.

Some people become overwhelmed with their goals, and the fears they develop stop them from achieving them. At some level, point in time, or in certain situations, remember everyone has felt afraid. If your identity is high, you will have the courage to go places other salespeople will not go. You will take chances and ask questions, unlike other salespeople. You need to be willing to share your knowledge and grow the other people on your team. You know a **"high I"** means you add high value to your team. This is where self-confidence comes from. This is also where the certainty of mind or the "zone" comes from. You should strive to build people up, and not tear them down. Be a human, not a crab! Help other people get what they desire in life. These are simple rules that will help you when you face tough customers. These are also simple rules that will help you personally push through the tough times in your own life.

Why do some people have **"low I"s?** There can be many reasons. However, just knowing a person has a **"low I"** will be the key of working around them. If you make them feel **"OK"**, then you can overcome their low self-esteem. People make their own choices, and you can never force someone to have a **"high I"**. A person has to become a **"high I"** on their own time, the same way they chose to have roles. You make choices to be a father, mother, manager, etc. There are exceptions to this rule, but we have a choice on our level in that particular role. We can choose to be great or mediocre, even bad, in that role. This is where your free will takes over. The one thing you also need to realize is that you can influence people's identity. People learn from other people. I had a colleague who taught me this on a daily basis. He always said, "You can't finish until you get started." Mr. Washington was a drill sergeant in the military. He rose to that rank because he had a **"high I"**. He always said he was *"locked and loaded"* when you spoke to him. It was his way of saying he was prepared. I am sure he failed many times in his life. He wanted people around him to succeed, because he knew if they were successful, he would be successful. I always knew he had a **"high I"** when we worked together. He made me feel **"OK"** when I spoke to him. I literally felt like I could accomplish anything when he spoke in our meetings. He was our inspiration for our sales team, and when I started working with the company, I sought him out. George was our number one salesperson. He had a very **"high I"**. He was always in the feeling of certainty. I now know all the traits that I teach, he already possessed. He was a winner. I yearned to be a better speaker, a better teacher, a better person. I later found out that was his goal also. He wanted everyone to become a better salesperson. He always left me better than he found me. Even though it has been over 16 years since I worked with Mr. Washington, I have never forgotten how great a salesperson and man he was.

Anyone can learn how to have a "**high I**". This is a teachable skill set. You just have to be confident in yourself and want people in your circle to push you to be a high performer.

Great golfers want to beat the course, not their opponent. They understand if they beat the course, they will also end up beating their opponent. Instead, wish for everyone to do the very best they can. Worry about yourself, and the rest will be taken care of for you. Focus on your outcome more than the rest of your peers. If you do that, then they will follow your example. If you do fail be gracious and learn why you failed. If you never quit, you will always get a second chance. These principles will help everyone around you in sales, and in life. Keeping a clear perspective on becoming a better person will also develop your sales skills. These seem to go hand in hand.

Chapter 8
Win-Win

Over the course of my career, I have interviewed hundreds of salespeople for the companies with which I have worked. I always asked the same final question at the end of each interview. That question was, "*If you had to use one word to encapsulate the most important part of the sales process, what would that word be?*" My pet answer to that question was "Empathy." I'd hung my hat on that word for many years. In other words, put yourself in the customer's shoes and see if you would buy. Then one day, I was conducting an interview with a lady who was selling advertising for the Yellow Pages® but was looking for a change in direction. When I asked her that same question at the end of the interview, she looked at me, shaking her head, and said, "I can't say it in one word, but I can in two: **"Win-Win."**

The words rolled out like distant thunder. It was a true epiphany for me. She went on to explain that the customer has to win, and the company has to win. How could something so simple be so basic and so easily missed?

When you feel like you got a great deal, you feel great. Likewise, if the company feels like they received a great deal, they feel great.

You will have to ask questions to make this happen, but make it your mission to strive for a "**win-win**".

In all honesty, how do we really know if we received a good deal? Sometimes when we buy things, we are unsure if we received a good deal. One thing to keep in mind is that a great deal is not always about a great price. A great deal could be a better delivery time. It could also be about inventory or quality. There are numerous reasons why people buy, and many factors for the customer to consider and weigh. It is your job to make sure they feel like they have won, keeping in mind that it cannot be a façade or some subterfuge to fool the customer. The customer genuinely has to win. They need to have a feeling of being **"OK"** that both parties can and did win. You do not have to stack the deck against them. If you are asking questions in the proper manner, they will tell you how you can win.

For example, I had a large deal once with a huge roofing company featuring a rust inhibitor. It was the **BASF** project of the year. They had received a quote from my competitor and were very happy with the price. I asked the **BASF** rep was there anything I could do to get the business. The rep and the distributor had a much better relationship than I had imagined.

I went to the roofing company to discuss the project, and the lead project manager could not have lunch with me that day. He told me that I would be joining someone else for lunch that day instead. I was disappointed but resolute in my conviction that I always try to make the customer happy, and I went to the lunch anyway. As luck would have it, my lunching companion was the owner of the company. Seizing the opportunity, I asked the owner numerous questions, but the lunch conversation was *all*

about him. I did not talk about the project at all. That afternoon, I prepared a quote and emailed it over and was quickly given the PO. I was ecstatic; however, shortly I learned my company would not accept the purchase order as received. While I was extremely frustrated, I remembered, **what you do not know will kill you.** The month prior, another salesperson cancelled a deal; as a result, we were sitting on the product. We were not going to win under these circumstances. My boss did not ask enough questions, and I failed to do the same. I had asked all the questions to the customer, but not a single question to my company. You cannot leave any rocks unturned. We are trained to blame others. It cannot possibly be us. You always need to put your team in a position to win. When I say a position to win, you have to make sure you can win. We were not in a position to win. I did not know all the facts. You have to always be looking for a way to win, and for your customer to win as well. If I'd communicated with my boss better, I would have closed the deal. You have to strive to get better every day, and winning will make you better. As they say, "Some days you get the bear, some days the bear gets you!"

Your customer must feel that they have received a winning deal. If he does not feel this way, you have no chance of repeat business. In tandem, your company must win. They are the ones who sign your paycheck. When you lean, you always lean toward the company. Some salespeople do not care if the company wins. These people eventually will find themselves at a company that believes they are insignificant. The sales profession, as it is! You never want an employer to feel that you are not a team player who will always advocate on their behalf.

To accomplish this, we must share the victory with the customer. We both have to win. It is critical that you understand this premise. It is a core fact of business sales today. We all want repeat business and referrals. That feeling a customer gets when they win, they share it with future purchasing agents and other customers.

Negative news circulates so much faster than good news. We all want to win. We should always want our customers to win. When the process is over, ask your customer if they feel like they received a good deal. The answer will shock you most of the time. This is also a great time to ask them, "Would you mind telling your friends?" You should never miss an opportunity for a referral if you did a great job and the customer feels like they have won. It is a perfect time to get your pen out and write down some leads from your customer.

I remember greeting a customer at my office, and they had my brochure in their hand. It was a photocopy of our company's brochure that was so expensive to produce that we only gave them to hot prospects. I asked this lady where she had received the brochure. She mentioned her neighbor purchased a home from us, and she saw it on a coffee table. She also explained that our prior customer did not want to part with the brochure; so instead, they photocopied the one they had. We all laughed, but we also found out how attached their neighbors were to their home.

This just shows you that you never know where your next customer comes from or how an existing relationship may benefit you in the future.

If their neighbor thought they had suffered a loss, they would have never shared the brochure. They wanted their friends to know how great a deal they received. There is a book called *Raving Fans*, by Ken Blanchard. He discusses this idea that your customer must win and stresses how you must blow your customer away.

I can only hope that in today's world, you would want to be different. Today, most customers feel shortchanged in the sales process. I am also sure that most customers do not feel like they have won. I want my customers to refer me to their friends, family, mailman, priest, rabbi, ex- and future ex-spouse. It is a must they win.

You want to be an ambassador for my company, and if you ever fall short, you need to figure out why. If you are asking questions properly, you will know why; the customer will tell you. A win-win will be the best feeling you can have in the sales process. We all want to win, and it is possible that we all can win.

If you take this one step further and make sure your team wins, there is even a greater reward. You will become a more profitable company, and your team will become proud to have you in their ranks. The sales team works harder for the other fellow teammates whom they like and trust!

If you employ this mindset, your team will have fewer turnovers and more tenure.

There is an old African proverb that says, "**If you want to go fast, go alone. If you want to go far, go together.**" If you are able to buy in to the wisdom in this proverb, it will help you achieve more together as a unit. We need to understand that great things are done with many. We will never truly be successful on our own. I have had tremendous help getting to where I am by many people. I have always played team sports, and even in golf it is a team effort. I always sought help in my game. I have always sought help in sales. There is also a cliché that states together we all achieve more.

TEAM
Together
Everyone
Achieves
More

If you really want to be a winner, you must start trusting your team. This starts with your management team. When conducting a sales seminar, I always ask my class to fill out a short survey before we start training. The question I pose is, "If your boss was running an election for the job they currently hold, would you re-elect them?" This is done anonymously and shared later that night with their boss. While it is not a popularity contest, they need to know how their sales team views them. You must lead from the front to be great. You need the respect of your team to do this; salespeople are far more likely to meet their goals when they have the support of their manager. It is a crucial piece of the formula for success. This is also a thin line to discern. How can we win with our customer if we are not acting like a team? Everyone is unmotivated by micromanagers, "A" players hate to be micromanaged. We will all grow with constructive criticism. You want to put our team and customer in a position to win, and it must start at the top.

Winning is one of those behaviors in life that becomes a habit. You have to appreciate the grind and discipline it takes to win. The greatest moment in sales will be when you win and your customer wins. There are pundits that will tell you not everyone can win. We know we all can win. There are just different levels of winning. The moment you put yourself first, and not the customer, you will fall short. We all know in sales we lose, but at what level? Pain is temporary, but quitting will last forever. Our life is filled with failures, especially in the sales industry.

Quitting can never be an option for you. Customers may not buy from you, but they will respect you if you stay the course. The main difference between winning and losing is marginal. The inches you need will be all around you. You must pay attention to what they are. There will be times when you want to tap out. You must keeping pushing the envelope.

Never be afraid to make a decision. The first step in every situation is to decide to do something. I meet hundreds of people that want to write a book. We all are certainly capable of writing a book, but we must take the first step in order to actually finish it. It took me 15 years to make the first step. I have surrounded myself with a team to execute my plan. The main reason I wrote this book was because I wanted to leave people better than I found them. There are people that are narcissistic and will not want you to win. The main thing you need to know is how to recognize those people. The team will not win unless they are working together as a unit. A great leader once said, "You do not have to like your teammates, but you must do your job." The clarity will surface when everyone is doing their job. It is fine to call people out when they are not; just make it a gracious and palatable discussion. At the beginning of this book, you read that 90% of salespeople will not do the things outlined on these pages. There is no need to point fingers at anyone on your team, because in doing so three fingers are pointing back at you.

It will be hard changing your life and learning how to win. When you will start to doubt yourself, stay the course. If you were not a risk taker, you would not be in the sales industry. It is necessary to get the losers out of your life. It is easy to lose, but more difficult to win. When you start this journey, people may be skeptical and not see what you see. You must keep the blinders up and align yourself with the winners. The greatest investment you will ever make will be in yourself. Most of the people that lose are victims. Do not mess up an apology with an excuse. Just be accountable to yourself and your team so we all can win.

So the question looms, why do we want our customer to win? Why not? The feeling of losing will always trump the feeling of winning. It is the persistence that will help us win. We need to make our customers feel **"OK".** You will earn as much as you invest into yourself, your team, and your customer.

We all have to come to the realization that we have to give as much as we get. One thing is clear: profitability is king. Our jobs will cease to exist without profit. There is equal footing when the value outweighs the cost. This formula is what creates a WIN-WIN. We all have overpaid for things in our lives, and the feeling that gives us feels like we have been taken advantage of. When you ask questions of your customer, it will help you establish value. My father always said, "A quick nickel is better than a slow dime any day." It has taken me 20 years to learn that philosophy. If your customer feels like they won, then you have won. The customer will tell everyone how great of a deal they received. You will create a new fan of your company. We all can win, and when your team embraces that concept, your sales volume will increase.

Chapter 9
Attitude

As we get closer to the end of the book, the last two chapters will be important. These skills have a compound effect and will each build upon the skill set explained in the chapter before. This book was intended to be a short read, which would help everyone become better at sales. We have discussed strategies, questions, and overcoming objections. These are all things you can do to help your customer. You can do everything we have discussed thus far, but if you do not have the right **attitude,** nothing will work. Your actions and your attitude are two things that you have complete control over.

If you were to ask some of the top salespeople in the country, attend many sales seminars, and survey over one hundred customers about their experiences, they would all say that the single most important quantity of a salesperson is a positive attitude. You must be in the state of **certainty**, and then your attitude will be positive.

I love to laugh, and great things happen to me when I am smiling. The first day I met one of the women on my sales team, you could tell she was a "Rainmaker". She was a **"glass is half full"** kind of person. Everyone on the team wanted to be around her. She always made her customers feel **"OK"**. The amazing thing about her was her attitude (I guess when you have a name like Faith, you have to be positive!).

Great salespeople migrate toward each other. Faith would walk across the room smiling, and you could feel the energy around her. From the first question she asked me, it was clear that she was an "interested", not just an "interesting" person. She really got it, and people liked being around her. I had many conversations with her about other sales staff members and myself. I jokingly called her the "interrogator". She was a pure example of "Can I ask you a question?" One day I found out her son was battling a brain tumor. I also found out she had a tough childhood. She still came in every day laughing and smiling. The main difference in her situation was she chose a persistent positive attitude instead of allowing herself to be a victim. Her attitude was as good as anyone I have ever coached in my lifetime. I always felt **"OK"**. We always laughed and joked around. She made you want to laugh.

When you see someone smile, it becomes contagious. Everyone loves being around positive people. The selling process is naturally full of rejection, and how you handle this will determine how successful you will be. It is imperative you have a great attitude. Sure, there are some days when you have to fake it, but you will see that a great attitude (even if sometimes forced) breeds success. If your attitude is great, then the people around you will follow suit.

I always made it "mandatory" to laugh in my sales meetings (that is a joke, folks!). I want my team to have a great time and enjoy being in a meeting.

They say there is never a good time for a meeting (you are probably nodding your heads in agreement!). We all are busy, so it is important to make the meeting worthwhile. In purposeless meetings, people struggle to stay focused, their attention slips into an abyss, and it is hard to revive their floating attitude once lost. Some people conduct meetings just to hear their own voice! A bad meeting has the power to give your sales team a bad attitude. It is critical you keep them upbeat and valuable. Do the world a favor: make a commitment today to avoid holding purposeless meetings for this reason!

Here is another idea: feed your team! Take a break every 45 minutes to give your team a breather. The mind will only absorb what the rear can withstand. Give your team every possible advantage for their attitude to remain positive and forward thinking.

A bad attitude is like cancer. It will spread unless you kill it. Do not let anyone around you have a bad attitude. Keep everyone positive, and positivity will spread. It all starts with the person and their self-development. The one thing you have the power to control every day is your attitude.

As a sales professional, you must "sharpen your axe" if you want to be great. "Axe" in this context is your skill set. You need to rest it, sharpen it, and swing it. You have to take time off and smell the roses. Every day for at least fifteen minutes, you need to take some "me" time. Drop what you are doing and take a break. This break will refresh you daily.

We all develop bad habits. **Some specifically** love to gossip, linger online, and so on. You know these hazards exist, so guard your time and mind fiercely and try to avoid them.

The road less traveled is filled with folks who have incredibly positive attitudes. These folks are almost always on top, so challenge yourself everyday to say or do something positive.

If you like to play golf (and you know I do), then do it. If you like to shop, do it. The late coach Jim Valvano said you should laugh, cry, and think every day. He said that was a full day. I agree with him. We should laugh every single day and find someone who can make us laugh.

The best sales teams ever assembled had some great times together. If you cannot make people laugh, learn how. If you are genuine, it will come natural. Walk in the office smiling, and they will smile also.

Most of the sales teams below their numbers have bad attitudes. Maybe not everyone on the team, but there are always a few bad apples who are not happy. There is a saying, **"It is easier to retrain than give birth**." Most sales managers feel totally different. They would much rather start fresh and hire someone without bad habits. However, because of the time and money it costs to rehire, that is a misguided mentality. We must put a value on that team member and hold the team and ourselves accountable as to why we are not hitting our goals.

When I was a sales manager, I always kept a box of **M&Ms**® in my office. If I had a salesperson struggling, I would drop them on their desk. I believe it is a polite way to make them realize they need to make more sales. If your sales person really cares about their job, they know exactly where they stand.

There is no need to micromanage a struggling salesperson. This generally makes the situation worse. Instead, ask how you can help. Ride along with them, and help close business. Help instill a good attitude so they reach their personal goals. It is your job to find out what those goals are for each member of your team.

Often, people have goals they may not be aware of, and that might not be part of their overall sales plan. Sometimes they were so caught up in trying to make their numbers, they would forget that those numbers reflected the success, or failure, of their own well-being. It is very important you keep an open dialogue with team members and managers on a weekly basis to see how you can help them reach their goals.

Great leaders lead from the front. If your salespeople do not like you, then the onus is on you. You do not need to be soft, but at the same time you should not be disliked. Treat your salespeople like they are your customers. If our customers did not like you, would you be successful? This is a rhetorical question, and we all know the answer. The cheapest thing we can give people is kindness; the easiest, most powerful thing to say is **"Thank you."** However, we must hold our salespeople accountable for their behaviors or actions. When you become an expert at leading, you will have knowledge of the answers to the questions that will inevitably come to the forefront.

Also remember:

What gets measured gets done.

This is a team dynamic, and everyone has to do their job. There are always tough conversations we need to have with our team, but there are also always ways to motivate people to produce. Have you noticed that when great teams win, they always thank the coach? You have to constantly let your team know that you are in the boat with them and that the burdens, as well as the accomplishments, are shared.

Success always starts with the right attitude in life. We are all creatures of our environment. If we have a poor work environment, people will reflect that poor environment. Have team meetings where there is an opportunity to have an open dialogue concerning how we can close more business and make our team and customers feel "**OK**".

Never treat your sales team any differently than the customer, because they emulate what they see. Salespeople have a propensity to become complacent, and it is the job of the manager to keep them motivated. This can mean different things to different people. We are always selling ourselves to the human race. One of the clichés out there is **"Attitude determines altitude."** We all want to win, but are we willing to take the steps needed to get results?

Set the proper environment, and be willing to change direction if you are not seeing the desired results. Great leaders can change directions quickly and recognize when they need to do that. We all know the definition of insanity---doing the same thing over and over and expecting a different result. Make it a point to change the behaviors in your office if things become constant or grow stale. It is critical we try different things to find what will increase attitudes. You are accountable as a leader to make sure your team is put in a position to win. Your team has to be prepared to win, and as the leader, it is your responsibility to foster that belief in your team that they can, and will win.

Make it a point to keep total clarity with your team. It helps everyone to communicate on a weekly basis. It could be in a passing conversation or over lunch. Ask the question, "What would you do if you were in my position?" You are always the final decision-maker, but **"none of us is as smart as all of us!"** When your salespeople feel they have input, their attitude will remain high. They will feel heard, and as the manager, you will feel in the loop; it is a win-win!

Everyone wants to have a great attitude, but do we each know what it takes? It is hard to do sometimes, but we must. We must fight to stay in a positive frame of mind every single day. The day will finish like it started most of the time. We can influence what happens most of the time by our attitude.

So the question becomes, why spend so much time on attitude? The main reason is, you have to be in the right frame of mind to succeed. It is the one of the few things you have the most control of in the sales arena. You can be conditioned to be positive all day long with practice. You should surround yourself only with people that have the right attitude. You can never let your customer see you sweat. You must remain on point and always be positive. The most important thing I found out about being in this frame of mind is that there are so many things to be positive about. This pertains to sales, as well as management. There is a saying, **"Some will, some won't, who cares, next!"** Focus on your circle of influence, and remove the emotion. In the grand scheme of things, what you are worried about right now will not matter in three years or less. We all naturally focus on what is immediately in front of us. When your attitude is right, the world is a better place as an added byproduct. A great attitude is to be passed on, and people will start to buy from your team because of their energy.

Most of the time, there is a direct correlation between a struggling sales force and a collective bad attitude. If this is the case with your team, spend time thoroughly assessing their attitude. Some people believe what was told to them in a negative way, and they believe it for a long time. When you face a tough challenge, you have to believe you can overcome it; otherwise, you will live in a continual place of doubt.

Steve Jobs was fired from the very company he started. He had the right attitude, because he was certain he was doing the right things. If he would have quit, Pixar would have never been created. He would have never changed the world for the better. I am not asking you to change the world; just yourself. We all must believe that we are doing the right things to achieve our goals. One saying for you to remember is, **"Stars only shine in the dark".** It is critical that you have the right attitude to get the job done. The greatest power you have is the control of your mind. You can choose to believe whatever you want to believe. This also pertains to your attitude. People's perception is their own reality. If you decide to be negative, you will be negative. If you decide to be positive, you will be positive. Most people do not want you to solve their problem; they just need you to listen. Negative people are contagious. Remove the problem as quickly as you can. Let's go back to chapter one and remember the importance of being responsive. We may never be able to change someone's attitude, but we can influence them. If we can provide a paradigm shift for them, they may see what we see. High performance people always have a positive attitude. This is difficult, because we deal with a great deal of rejection. Embrace rejection with vigor, because your attitude will be right. The more people you are around with a positive attitude, the more positive your attitude will become. It is contagious as a negative attitude. Make it your purpose to speak to customers and make them laugh and feel "**OK**". It will be your attitude that sets you apart.

My goal when I meet someone is to really get to know them. I love to hear people's stories. It truly inspires me to learn from people. My father owned a supermarket and was a social animal. When he became a developer, he had the skill set to sell property. He had studied people for over ten years, and their personalities. He always had a positive attitude and generally wanted to help people. I remember so much laughter in the store. My father really made people feel "**OK**". I watched him as a child get up in the middle of the night and open the supermarket to get medicine for someone who had a sick child. I observed him pump gas at three in the morning because someone needed to drive over 40 miles to the hospital. The next morning, his attitude was always positive in front of his customers. I knew he was tired, but he smiled. He was laying the foundation of my sales career. I understand what really being positive means. This book was written to help people become better. It will start with the right attitude. I hope you are always positive.

Chapter 10

What do you think about going ahead with this today?

This is the final chapter, and it will serve as the end cap to the skills and knowledge you have acquired throughout this book. **Can I ask you a question?** If I could show you how to close 50% more business, would you be interested? Of course you would. If you practice everything covered in this book, you will start to see positive results over time. As you close more, the more successful you will be. At some point down the line, you will become a true "rainmaker". But do not take my word for it; you will know when that moment arrives.

We let fear stand in the way of asking for things, going after that proverbial "brass ring". If you remember, you have to get your fears out on the table.

When the final moment of a particular sales deal arrives, hold your hand out to shake the customer's hand and ask, "***What do you think about going ahead with this today?***" The customer will then let you know where you stand. If you did a great job, the answer will always be "yes", and you will gain new information to make traction going forward.

If you have left some part undiscovered, the customer will give you an objection. Your job will be to overcome those objections with questions. These questions will help you earn a "yes". If they say "no", you need to know why - so ask them! Be very careful how you ask this question. You can say, "Was it something I did not do? Was it me, as a person?" You have to be genuine and really ask some tough questions. "Was it the price?" This will help set the budget. These are some examples of questions that will help both you and the customer.

You should learn to love objections. As a true professional, there is nothing you cannot overcome. You have to be prepared for whatever answer they give. If they give you a question that you cannot answer, the fail-safe response is "That is a great question, why do you ask?" It will give you time to hear their response and what direction you need to go in. And **remember, not all customers are buyers**.

We all have had customers to whom we wish we would never have sold. You have to fall on your sword and make them feel **"OK"** just to get out of a poor decision. It is a fact that we cannot make everyone happy. I always say everything in life fails for two reasons only: (this is a broad-brush statement, but true) **communication** and **expectations**.

It is critical that you keep the path of communication open at all times. You remember, chapter one is being responsive. Most great salespeople gloss over the expectation in fear of losing a sale. It is your job as leaders to make sure that all items are covered and put on the table. We never want to add something that will keep us from closing more sales. David Sandler calls this **"painting seagulls."** You must never create objections. Trust me; customers are already masters at finding them on their own. In addition, why would you want to bring in an objection that could cost you business? The processes are tough enough without you helping the customer stall or derail the sale. Each step of the sales process matters. It is vital to be thorough, honest, and genuine. If you fail to do this, it will come back to bite you every single time.

Ask the customer, "Is there anything you still have a question about?" What you do not know throughout the sales process can blindside you. It is impossible to catch everything; however, if there is a pattern of the same problem, it is your responsibility to address it.

Asking the question, "What do you think about going ahead with this today?"

should always put you in a high point of leverage. This question will serve as a guide for asking additional questions to position you for success. Ask the question at the end of a conversation or presentation to see if the customer is on the same page. This will help you evaluate to see if you have missed covering an important aspect about the product in the process. It will truly help your customer see the value in your presentation. Another way to assess the temperature of a customer is to ask the following scale question:

"On a scale of one to ten, where are we at on getting a purchase order or contract signed on my product?"

You can tailor this to whatever you are selling. It is a simple, yet effective question on summing up the close. If you are a manager, follow up with your team to see what their customers' answers were if they lost the sale. If you do this all the time, your sales will continue to increase. This may sound like common sense, but so many forget to make the final "ask".

You must always remember to ask a customer to buy.

It is one of the main reasons a sales professional's close ratio could be low. Many people do not ask for the sale. It may be perceived by some as "old school", but it still holds true. You have to place your "order" if you want to get served. No one gets married if they do not ask. You have to, 100% of the time, ask this question.

Do not put pressure on yourself to rush to the close. When you master the first nine parts outlined in this book, when the time is right, you will absolutely know when to ask. There will also be sales presentations when a close may not be available. If you have not covered all your bases, you will find you are wasting your time. At times it may feel confusing, but your customer will always let you know if your timing is right. Sometimes you will make sales months down the road. If you stay in contact and follow up with your customer, you will close more business. The answer to that question tells you how well you have done your job. You have to commit to asking your customer for the sale.

This is the one thing that most sales professionals are not doing in the workforce. It will differentiate you from the masses.

Conclusion

I would like to thank everyone who asked me to write this book over the years, and who had a hand in shaping me as a great salesperson. I never would have gotten this far without the help of so many. All the information in this book was taught to me by other people; I just paid close attention. There are two types of people you remember: **those who go through life, and those who go through life and pay attention.**

When I became skilled at doing these things outlined in *Can I Ask You A Question?*, I became a great salesperson. I was just a great conversationalist when all this started. My father was a great salesperson because he put his customers first. He was truly concerned about them. He was always and still is genuine. He was never afraid of failing or letting his children fail.

My bosses were always about team, or at least the great ones were. They wanted everyone to win. My people skills were gained by working in my father's supermarket, starting when I was five years old. My father always made people feel **"OK"**. I was always mad because he made us work all the time. I know now why; he did not have a choice. We were always taught, **If it is to be - it's up to me**. I see people in today's world that are not even slightly responsive. We are in a society where we want all the credit but do little of the work. It is hard to give people credit; it is not in our selfish nature. We want to win at all costs. Is it really worth winning if we destroy our team? You will win sometimes, but it will not be on a regular basis.

I had a fear about writing a book, but if I did not share these simple things, I would not be helping people get better. I also let fear stand in my way. We all have fear, but it is how we handle that fear that makes us the person we become.

I look back at all my failures, and there are many. It is easy to connect the dots when we look in the past. I have always prided myself on being right. I have found through experience that being right is not that important. I believe helping people get what they want is far more important.

I have a true purpose and calling to help salespeople be better. It is a driving force for me to share all the knowledge, tips, and observations I have gained over the years and spread that information around. I was told that the graveyard is full of your unused value. I never want to be the person that never shared what I have been taught. I look at all the companies I have worked with and understand that I can help people get so much more out of their lives from those experiences taught to me. If this makes someone a better person, better salesperson, better manager, well then I have accomplished what I set out to do.

More than anything else, I hope these things, thoughts, and observations leave you better than I found you.

Thanks to you all for spending your precious time reading my book. It has been a pleasure writing about a subject so close to my heart. These simple ten skills will increase your skill set and help you close more business in the future. I honestly believe these steps have helped me understand the true sales process and really connect with people. If you will commit to these principles, you will start to see results. I encourage you to keep this book with you at all times and use it as a true resource or playbook. It will serve as a reminder to always fall back on the true fundamentals of the sales process. We all need reminding what is truly important in the arena of sales (and in life!). We all are only as good as our resources. I remind myself of these principles on a daily basis. In closing, make a difference in your life in all aspects. Just remember to say one thing daily:

"Can I Ask You A Question?"

Special Thanks to

My bride Carla Robinson, Kyra Robinson, Dalton Robinson, Thomas and Sandra Robinson, Cotton, Emerson Manning, Charles Clarke, David Sandler, Zig Ziglar, Larry and Evelyn Robinson, Charlie and Donna Britt, Uncle Donald, Mack Briggs, George Washington, Gary Eubanks, Billy Lewis, Ken Gerrard, Randy Miller, Irv Parnell, Ryan Fitzgerald, Howard Stevens, Bill Rogers, Faith Stegall, Leslie Thomasson, Larry "The Pro" Gregory, Henry Lindley, Buzz, Rick Laws, Benjy Adams, Dave Tucker, Barry Connor, Bill Salmon, KO, Ronnie Beal, Keith Gunther, Frollie Hughes, Tommy Robinson, Danny Clemmons, Coach Byrd, SGT Major Williams, Col. Moss, Nick Broccolo, Fred Damuth, Dink, Ike Howard, Jerry King, Fred Deluca, Jack the Cookie Man, Harold Johnson, Tug Rainey, and all the teachers in my life. I understand none of the following would have been possible without the help of so many.

I hope you are always OK.